Blended Learning

Creating Learning Opportunities for Language Learners

Debra Marsh

CAMBRIDGE
UNIVERSITY PRESS

CAMBRIDGE UNIVERSITY PRESS
Cambridge, New York, Melbourne, Madrid, Cape Town,
Singapore, São Paulo, Delhi, Mexico City

Cambridge University Press
32 Avenue of the Americas, New York, NY 10013-2473, USA

www.cambridge.org

First published 2012

Printed in the United States of America

ISBN 978-1-107-91697-5 Paperback

Book layout services: Page Designs International

Table of Contents

Introduction

Learning a foreign language presents different challenges for different people in different contexts. The reasons for learning a foreign language are as diverse as the ways different individuals approach the task of learning new vocabulary, figuring out new grammar rules, listening, reading, and speaking in a language other than their native language. A range of methods and approaches are often used to introduce new language, and a variety of classroom management techniques are employed to maximize practice opportunities. In short, there is no one way to learn a language, just as there is no one way to teach it. But, are there optimal conditions for effective language learning? What conditions are required in an "effective" learning environment?

Much research time and resources have been dedicated to examining these questions. "Optimal" conditions for effective language learning have been identified and characterized in a number of studies, but the most general and most cited (Egbert & Hanson-Smith, 1999) include the following:

1. Learners interact in the target language with an authentic audience.

2. Learners are involved in authentic tasks.

3. Learners are exposed to and are encouraged to produce varied and creative language.

4. Learners have opportunities to interact socially and negotiate meaning.

5. Learners have enough time and feedback.

6. Learners are guided to attend mindfully to the learning process.

7. Learners work in an atmosphere with an ideal stress/anxiety level.

8. Learner autonomy is supported.

The majority of foreign language teaching still takes place in the classroom, and as language teachers, we know from experience that achieving the "optimal" conditions as just presented poses a significant challenge in most foreign language teaching situations where students have limited opportunities to actively engage in using the target language. Surrounded by native language speakers, students rarely have the opportunity to enter the world of the target language, despite our best efforts to introduce communicative, authentic language tasks into out classrooms.

In any one classroom, a teacher can be faced with students who all have their own individual learning preferences, who come from different backgrounds, and who have different priorities and reasons for learning a language. Any group of students can often be of mixed ability with different goals or learning styles. Appropriateness of task can represent a significant challenge in these circumstances. Teachers know from experience that if a language level in a task is too easy, some students are unlikely to improve; if the task is too difficult, some students may simply give up. Similarly, tasks that do not address a student's interests or learning style may fail to motivate, which is essential to language learning.

Time is limited in the classroom, and although teachers are well aware of the need to provide their students with opportunities to practice the language in different and varied contexts, this is sometimes just not feasible given timetabling constraints.

As language teachers we understand that to serve the needs of our learners, we need to create an environment that most closely resembles actual use of the target language. In attempting to achieve the "optimal" learning environment, we have a number of resources and tools available. Recording devices, video players, newspapers, and language laboratories all provide different and varied access to content. We can employ a variety of activity types with group work and pair work, collaborative learning and independent learning to engage our learners in communicative language practice. We all try to address the need for personalized learning through the introduction of self-study resources designed for independent study.

In other words, as language teachers, although we may not have been aware of the term, we have always used a "blend" of teaching approaches in order to provide as rich a learning environment as possible for our learners. Blended learning is therefore not a new concept. What is new is the range of different learning opportunities and environments made possible today through the use of technology to support learning and teaching. What is also new is the "expectation" of our learners to use technology in and out of the classroom as part of the learning process.

In the sections that follow, we will consider how blended learning can help achieve the "optimal" language learning environment. We will examine the criteria and factors that will help you choose the appropriate "blend" for your students, and we will also consider the different teacher and learner roles that make for effective blended language learning.

1

A "Blended" Solution for Language Learning

Blended learning refers to a mixing of different learning environments. The phrase has many specific meanings based upon the context in which it is used. Blended learning gives learners and teachers a potential environment to learn and teach more effectively.

http://blendedlearning506no.wikispaces.com/Secande+Life

Herein, any reference to blended learning assumes the continued use of face-to-face teaching as a basic building block of the learning experience, enriched and enhanced by the integration of the Internet and other teaching and learning technologies into studies undertaken both in and out of the classroom. This integration should happen with the mediation and support of the teacher and, as with any materials used, should reflect and work toward the learning aims and needs of all learners.

Blending different learning methods, approaches, and strategies is not new

The most effective teaching and learning have always involved the use of different methods, approaches, and strategies to maximize knowledge acquisition and skills development. Good teachers will always use more than one method or approach in their teaching, and good learners will always combine different strategies in their learning. Good programs of study combine lectures, seminars, group projects, placements, and so on to offer students a variety of different learning opportunities. "Traditional" distance learning courses have long provided blended learning through a combination of self-access content (print/video/TV/radio and face-to-face/telephone support).

The practice of blending learning is, therefore, not a new way of teaching, nor is it a single method of learning. The term *blended learning* first appeared around 2000 and was at that time often associated with simply supplementing traditional classroom learning with self-study e-learning activities. More recently, the pedagogic value of providing blended learning opportunities has received significant attention, and the term has evolved to encompass a much richer set of learning approaches and environments. Today *blended learning* can refer to any combination of different methods of learning, different learning environments, different learning styles. In short, the effective implementation of blended learning is essentially all about making the most of the learning opportunities and tools available to achieve the "optimal" learning environment.

Language learning, the classroom, online content, and Web 2.0

Computers have been used in language teaching since the 1960s, and teachers have been blending face-to-face instruction with various kinds of technology-mediated language learning for decades. However, the impact of CALL (computer-assisted language learning) has been relatively modest. This has been mainly due to the absence of technology appropriate to the specific needs of language learners. This all changed with the arrival of the Internet, which provides second language learners with immediate access to the worldwide community of English language speakers, and to authentic resources through its billions of interconnected Web pages. The Internet, in particular the emergence of Web 2.0, represents a powerful medium to teach and learn foreign languages.

Although, the majority of foreign language teaching is still primarily conducted face-to-face in classrooms, the rapid growth in the use of learning technologies, particularly the use of the Internet and Web-based communication, is providing language teachers and students with many more opportunities to explore the most suitable mix of teaching and learning styles for a given task. Network-mediated learning and computer-assisted language learning offer directions that have attracted attention and are now considered an important component or venue in any language learning curriculum.

Blended language learning (i.e., integrating the use of technology into classroom-based learning and teaching) is still a relatively new concept, but recent research (Pena-Sanchez & Hicks, 2006; Stracke, 2005; and Stracke, 2007a) appears to indicate that when "appropriately" implemented, blended learning can significantly improve the learning experience. In an online poll of 300 CALL-related language teachers from 36 countries, Ruthven-Stuart (2003) found that 98 percent agreed that one of the roles of a computer was "a complement to classroom teaching."

The following strengths of blended language learning have been identified.

- provides a more individualized learning experience
- provides more personalized learning support
- supports and encourages independent and collaborative learning
- increases student engagement in learning
- accommodates a variety of learning styles

- provides a place to practice the target language beyond the classroom
- provides a less stressful practice environment for the target language
- provides flexible study, anytime or anywhere, to meet learners' needs
- helps students develop valuable and necessary twenty-first century learning skills

Many teachers use these tools to enhance their students' learning. For example, word processing software is used to experiment with collaborative writing, self-assessment, and peer assessment – a function that can also be taken outside the classroom by using wikis. Students are encouraged to use instant messaging to practice conversation skills and forums for discussion on topics of interest. The Internet is used for research on class projects. Some students have their own blogs to practice writing and engage with an audience. Blogs are being used to create learner diaries to foster reflective practices and help develop skills and strategies that are vital to successful independent learners. Class blogs are used to summarize the day's learning for absentees and provide writing practice for the "scribe" of the day. Through the use of these tools, teachers and learners are already engaging in the blended learning experience, perhaps without even realizing it.

Online learning/teaching environments can provide for different ways of learning and the construction of a potentially richer learning environment that provides fresh approaches to learning, thereby allowing for different learning styles, as well as greater diversification in and greater access to learning. Such learning environments should supplement or complement traditional face-to-face learning environments or, on the other hand, may provide a complete learning package that requires little face-to-face contact. Without a doubt, all teaching in the very near future will be supported by more or less digital- or net-based flexible solutions in the educational organization. Thus, the important question to ask ourselves now is how should we blend?

2 | *Finding Your Blend*

The most important aim of a blended learning design is to find the most effective and efficient combination of learning modes for the individual learning subjects, contexts, and objectives. The focus is not to choose "the right" or "the best," "the innovative" as opposed to "the traditional"; but to create a learning environment that works as a whole.

(Neumeier 2005, 164–65)

The concept and practice of blending learning opportunities is not new, but in today's digital age, what is new is the range of possible components in a blend. Blended learning, when well understood and implemented, has the potential to support deep and meaningful learning, but simply mixing information technologies with face-to-face learning is not sufficient to exploit the potential of blended learning. When considering blended learning, there is no single perfect blend, nor is there a set or simple formula for making a "good" blend. There is, however, a number of important factors essential to achieving an "effective" blend.

Complementarity

It is important for the different "ingredients" of the blend to complement each other. A mismatch between the various components can lead to confusion and frustration on the part of the students and increased workload for the teacher who has to attempt to bring the disparate components together to achieve a coherent learning experience.

The starting point for establishing complementarity is to identify the learning outcomes, identify your students' needs, and identify the different, potential components available to you. At this point, you should then be able to identify how best these learning outcomes and needs can be supported by the different components available to you.

Pedagogically sound learning materials

The choice of materials is critical. Interactivity and multimodality are crucial to demonstrating to learners that technology has something to offer them within the language learning framework. Teachers need to evaluate educational materials such as software programs carefully and use only those materials that are methodologically sound. Students like to use different media. Newer technologies and older media (i.e., CD-ROMs) both have a place in blended language learning where learners can choose the medium that best suits their needs. Teachers need to vary the usage of such media to accommodate student needs.

Support

In any blended learning context in which technology supported self-study is central to the blend, learners will require support in three important ways: academic, affective, and technical.

Academic

In and out of class, students can struggle with the concepts and constructs of language and of learning. In class, the teacher is on hand to answer questions as they arise. This can be carried through to the online medium by having forums for the different activities where students are invited to ask about issues they find difficult. By doing this in a forum (which supports peer-to-peer and group interaction) and not via e-mail (which only encourages student-to-teacher interaction), other members of the class are empowered and encouraged to respond to their peers' questions. This can provide considerable satisfaction for the person answering the question. As well as helping the questioner on an immediate level, it also reinforces the idea that the teacher is not the "source of all knowledge" and creates a sense of community and peer support in general.

Affective

Interaction in the classroom provides an excellent medium to support students who might be struggling with the coursework or feel a bit lost, especially when working at home alone. The use of student blogs and learner progress reporting available with many learning management systems provides the teacher with a good overview of who is falling behind or feeling isolated. It also offers the opportunity to provide support on these levels without drawing attention to it in class, particularly with quieter students who often get overlooked in the busy classroom. Web 2.0 tools, that is, tools that promote the communicative use of technology (e.g., forums and blogs), are vital in supporting the learner community.

Technical

Whenever technology is involved – and this is the case in any learning environment – things can go wrong. Technical support in vital, and teachers and students need this support in order to feel comfortable in what is a new and challenging experience.

3 | *The Teacher's Role in the Blend*

Students can't be "taught" – they can only be helped to learn. In a student-centered classroom, our role is to help and encourage students to develop their skills, but without relinquishing our more traditional role as a source of information, advice, and knowledge. In a student-centered classroom, the teacher and the students are a team working together.

(Jones 2007, 25)

The teacher's role has always been central to providing a structured and engaging teaching and learning environment. The classroom/face-to-face teaching component remains central to blended language learning, and the role of the teacher in the blended learning environment remains indispensable. Technology can only achieve so much, and the teacher has to be the motivating, organizing force to the integration of students' online and classroom learning. Many features of the teacher's role remain unchanged in the blended learning environment. The teacher continues to encourage and motivate, guide and monitor progress, give feedback, boost confidence, and maintain motivation.

Promoting student-centered learning in the classroom

Blended learning is, by it very nature, "student-centered." As the classroom is the "familiar" learning environment for our students, then it follows that this is the starting point for promoting student-centered learning practices.

In student-centered teaching, we focus our planning, our teaching, and our assessment around the needs and abilities of our students. The main idea behind the practice is that learning is most meaningful when topics are relevant to the students' lives, needs, and interests and when the students themselves are actively engaged in creating, understanding, and connecting to knowledge.

In a student-centered classroom, students

- are involved in the learning process.
- don't depend on their teacher all the time.
- communicate with each other in pairs and small groups.
- value each other's contributions.
- cooperate.

- learn from each other.
- help each other.

In a student-centered classroom, the teacher

- helps to guide students.
- manages their activities.
- directs their learning.
- helps students develop their language skills.

Facilitating the blend

Blended learning promises all the advantages of allowing you to tailor your classroom time to the language areas best suited to face-to-face teaching, and providing you with the flexibility to select those areas based on your students' needs. Our students' computer skills are generally very good, so the "technical" and actual use of computer technology does not usually present a major challenge when introduced into our students' learning environment.

The teacher's role in facilitating the blend should not be underestimated. Using the technology effectively for learning often requires training and support. Students need to adopt and use learning strategies that are different from what they are used to in the more traditional, face-to-face classroom environments. For example, in the classroom, students' learning activities are usually structured and adjusted according to individual and group need by the teacher. But in blended learning, there is more reliance on student self-directed learning. The teacher, therefore, needs to help students take on the responsibility for their own learning.

Hints and tips

- Plan the blend carefully; consider the learning outcomes, the technology available, and the institutional constraints.
- Build in flexibility and be prepared to adapt to your students' needs.
- Build in time in the early stages of the course to introduce students to the technology and learning approach.

Encouraging autonomous and collaborative learning

Blended learning allows students to decided when and where they want to study. This flexibility can present some difficulties to students who have poor time management skills and who are not used to working autonomously. It is your role as the teacher to help your students develop the skills they require to work independently, particularly if this is the first time they have learned a language in a blended learning environment.

Hints and tips

- Allocate some class time for developing learning-to-learn skills, particularly in the early stages of the course.
- Create an online forum for discussion and advice.
- Explore questions, such as: What did you do to help yourself remember those new words? Who has a new tip for finding the main idea when you read a passage? How did you figure out what was going to happen next? What helps you listen and remember?
- Encourage students to work in pairs or buddy groups to support each other online.
- Create language tasks that require students to work together in small groups, either face-to-face or online.
- Help your students identify their own strengths and weaknesses, and encourage them to work with the appropriate activities online.
- Underscore the importance of deadlines and the how the online and classroom activities are integrated; for example, "X needs to be done by Wednesday in order for you to get the most out of the lesson that afternoon."
- Help students design their first study plan. Let them know how many hours of study are required per week and encourage them to identify the times when they will be able do part or all of that study.

Creating a supportive online community

Blended language courses aim to foster autonomous learning, but autonomous learning does not mean students are learning on their own. An online community can provide exactly the encouragement needed when students face their computer screen outside of the classroom. You will need to find ways to create a friendly, social online environment, which is essential for successful online learning.

Hints and tips

- Encourage your students to complete a profile online so they can get to know each other quickly.
- Create a "Café" forum where students can "meet" online and talk about things other than the course.
- Create a "Questions" forum and have your students post questions on activities. Encourage them to reply to each others' questions rather than relying only on the teacher's contributions.

Managing and facilitating online interaction

Depending on the technology used, blended learning can provide opportunities for genuine interaction online. One of the simplest communication tools is a forum, or bulletin board. Your role as the teacher is to monitor this interaction and decide how best to manage it, but remember your role is to facilitate and not direct or lead the interaction. How you approach your role as e-moderator will have a significant bearing on the online learning experience of your students.

Hints and tips

- Start a new discussion linked to the topic of the current unit at the beginning of every week.
- Every week give a different student the responsibility of facilitating a discussion in the forum.
- Encourage your students to contribute to the online discussions at least three times a week.
- Ask your students to start new discussions relevant to their own interests in the forum.
- Monitor student activity online and be prepared to send private e-mails to encourage the shyer students to participate. Similarly, if there is a student who appears overly outspoken, ask that person (privately) to wait a few responses before contributing again.

The Student's Role in the Blend

*The pedagogical rationale behind BLL [blended language learning]
is the desire to allow for a higher degree of learner independence in the
teaching and learning of second/foreign languages.*

(Stracke 2007b, 1)

It is often overlooked that students need time to adapt to and develop in a new learning environment. Supporting students through this transition is crucial.

Managing and planning independent study time

Hints and tips

- Provide your students with a clear course plan. This should provide an overview of the course schedule, the start and finish dates of units, the start and finish dates of the four lessons within each unit, and the dates of the unit tests and final test. This should also include an estimate of weekly workload (e.g., two hours in class plus four hours online). Students then know they have to fit four hours of study around their other commitments.

- Encourage students to use this course plan as a basis for planning their own time. This will help them work regularly and steadily throughout the course and ensure that they are able to keep up with the rest of the class.

- Encourage students to take time to carefully work out the best times for them to study.

Learning independently

The online component of blended learning allows students to learn when and where they want. It offers students the complete flexibility to choose the time they study with no constraints of fixed "classroom" hours. However, this does mean that students will need to get used to working independently, making their own decisions, and taking responsibility for their own learning. In the early stages of the course, some students will need help and guidance as to when and how to make these decisions. It is important that students understand that this flexibility does not mean they can leave all the online work until the last minute (i.e., the week before their exam).

Hints and tips

- Build in class and online discussion time to provide this support.
- Review students' study plans regularly to ensure their planning is realistic.
- Monitor students' progress online to ensure they are keeping up with the activities set.

Working collaboratively online

A blended language course should provide students with the tools and the opportunities to interact with their classmates, and it is important that students learn to take full advantage of the online community.

Hints and tips

- Set up activities at the start of the course that help students understand that their classmates are there to help them, just as they are there to help their classmates. For example, create a "Getting Help" forum and encourage students to post any questions there. In the early weeks of the course, you may need to encourage students to answer each other's postings, but very quickly students will see the value of sharing knowledge and helping each other in this way.
- Set up project-type activities that require students to work in small groups to achieve a concrete learning outcome. This may be a presentation in class or an online wiki.

Reviewing and self-correcting

Many online learning materials are automatically "marked," so students receive an immediate "score." Achieving the correct answers provides students with a clear sense of progress and achievement, but students also need to know what to do when they get something wrong.

Hints and tips

- Help students monitor their own progress and identify their own strengths and weaknesses.

- Provide a list of reference materials for students to review and have them practice again the items they answered incorrectly.

- Encourage students to try activities again a day or two after they have done them to help them review and consolidate learning.

5 Designing Pathways for Blended Learning

"[B]lended" is not a single approach or a separate alternative to online/ classroom environments, but rather a flexible continuum of various language learning environments. In such a paradigm, there can be no definition of an "online task" that is separate from a "classroom task". The aim of blended learning is then to span this continuum, defining and describing tasks that encompass the different environments.

(Hinkelman 2005, 19)

The number of different ways to blend learning opportunities and environments are potentially limitless, and many different factors need to be considered in order to achieve a blend that is appropriate to the needs of our students. We, of course, need to consider the identified learning outcomes for our lessons and program of learning, but then we also need to take into account the constraints presented by timetabling and the number of classroom hours per week our students are expected to attend. In addition, we need to calculate the number of hours of independent study they are expected to do per week, and how much time, we as teachers, have to monitor and support online learning.

Consequently, there is no "one-size-fits-all blended pathway. However, there are a number of key steps, as outlined below, that teachers can follow. These simple steps provide a solid foundation upon which to develop a pathway suited to the needs of your students.

A pathway template and key principles

The pathway template is designed to provide your students with

- an effective and efficient use of classroom time.
- increased opportunities for using English outside of class.
- maximum opportunities for review and recycling for improved learning.

There are three parts to the pathway template:

1. Online: prepare for class
2. In class: focus on communication
3. Online: review, extend, and consolidate

1. Online: Prepare for Class

New vocabulary can be introduced and practiced before class.

One of the key roles of the teacher is to introduce and present new language. However, in the classroom, it is not always possible to ensure that all students have completely understood this new language. Some students require more time to grasp new concepts and language. Others need time to build confidence in how to use the language in context.

This part of the pathway allows students to explore and practice new language in their own time and at their own pace, according to their own personal learning needs, before class. Students, therefore, come to class better prepared and more confident in their ability to participate in classroom activities.

Students can be prepared for "real-life" native speaker interaction.

The more exposure students have to different contexts, voices, and accents, the more confident they will feel in the "real" world use of language.

Students can develop listening and reading skills in their own time and at their own pace.

Listening and reading are usually activities we prefer to do at our own pace. In "real life," we usually read on our own and in our own time. When we listen to something, we often have our personal reasons for doing so, reasons that may not be shared with someone else listening to the same thing.

Ideas

- Make good use of the wealth of resources available in the target language on the Internet. These resources are available in all media (text, video, audio, etc.) and provide your students with immediate access to authentic language use in context.

- Direct students to Web sites linked thematically to the classroom topic. Encourage them to read, listen, or watch the content on these Web sites and note down any new language. Tell students to look up any new vocabulary in their dictionaries and record it in a vocabulary notebook.

- Encourage students to work together online in a forum or a chat room to build a collaborative vocabulary notebook.

- Encourage students to work together to find more resources on the stated topic on the Internet. Students can work in small groups and then share the resources they find with other groups.
- Set up a collaborative, document-sharing area online and encourage students to share the resources they find.
- Set up an online discussion around the topic to be talked about in the next lesson. This may be done with a text chat tool or in real-time via an audio conferencing tool such as Skype.

2. In Class: Focus on Communication

Students can be prepared online to actively participate in personalized pair- and group-work activities in class.

In class, teachers can focus on communicative activities that encourage real language use through pair and group work.

Student-to-student interaction is maximized in the classroom.

As a result, there is more time in class to focus on communicative activities to develop students' speaking skills. This builds students' confidence in their ability to communicate in the "real" world and increases student motivation to learn.

Ideas

- Identify the pair- and group-work activities provided in the textbook you are using with your students. Use these as a basis for planning your class activities.
- Conduct a survey with your students to find out the topics that interest them.
- Encourage students to work together to prepare topic-based discussions for class.
- Allow groups of students to facilitate the class discussion, while you take a back seat and observe the interaction.

3. Online: Review, extend, and consolidate

Students can review and consolidate language in their own time and at their own pace.

Students learn in different ways and at different paces. At the end of the class, some students may feel less confident than others in their ability to use the new language. Communication and interaction activities need not only start and end in the classroom. These can also be continued online with the support of a variety of Web 2.0 tools, such as chat rooms, forums, blogs, wikis, and real-time audio and video conferencing applications such as Skype.

Students can be motivated and interest can be stimulated through "real-life" online interaction.

Students today are familiar with the concept forums, Skype, chat rooms, and blogs. Activities that promote the use of these tools can provide motivational interest and encouragement to students to go online and interact in the target language.

Students can develop writing skills in their own time and at their own pace.

Writing is a personal activity and one that can be developed and supported online through the use of blogs and wikis.

Ideas

- Encourage your students to set up their own English blog. Provide guided practice writing tasks to encourage students to post to their blogs on a regular basis.
- Encourage students to read each other's blogs and post comments.
- Set up a class wiki to which all students can post and comment.
- Set up project-based activities that encourage students to work together online to achieve a common outcome.

Template for Designing Blended Learning

Follow these four steps to start designing your own blended pathway.

1. Identify the learning outcomes for your classroom lesson.
2. Identify the activities for student to do **in** class.
3. Identify the activities for students to do online **before** class.
4. Identify the activities for student to do **after** class.

LEARNING OUTCOMES
1. Identify the learning outcomes for your classroom lesson.

FOCUS ON COMMUNICATION **IN CLASS**
2. Identify the activities for student to do **in** class.
Students are prepared online to actively participate in personalized pair- and group-work activities in class. Student-to-student interaction is maximized in the classroom.

PREPARE FOR CLASS **ONLINE**
3. Identify the activities for students to do online **before** class.
New vocabulary can be introduced and practiced before class. Students can be prepared for "real-life" native speaker interaction. Students can develop listening and reading skills in their own time and at their own pace.

REVIEW, EXTEND, AND CONSOLIDATE **ONLINE**
4. Identify the activities for student to do **after** class.
Students can review and consolidate language in their own time and at their own pace. Students can be motivated and interest can be stimulated through "real-life" online interaction. Students can develop writing skills in their own time and at their own pace.

References

Brodsky, M. May 2003. E-learning trends, today and beyond. *Learning and Training Innovations.*

Chapelle, C. *Computer Applications in Second Language Acquisition.* New York: Cambridge University Press, 2001.

Cheers, C. and P. Towndrow. 2002. "Blended language learning." Learners Together. Accessed January 2012. http://www.learnerstogether.net/ PDF/Blended-Language-Learning.pdf.

Egbert, J. and E. Hanson-Smith. *Call Environments: Research, Practice, and Critical Issues.* Alexandria, VA: TESOL, 1999.

Harvey, L. (2004–2011). Analytic quality glossary, Quality Research International. Accessed January 2012. http://www. qualityresearchinternational.com/glossary/.

Hinkelman, D. 2005. Blended learning: Issues driving an end to laboratory-based CALL. *JALT Hokkaido Journal* 9: 17–31. Accessed January 2012. http://www.jalthokkaido.net/jh_journal/2005/Hinkelman.pdf.

Jones, L. *The Student Centered Classroom.* New York: Cambridge University Press, 2007. Also available at http://www.cambridge.org/other_files/ downloads/esl/booklets/Jones-Student-Centered.pdf.

Neumeier , P. 2005. A closer look at blended learning – parameters for designing a blended learning environment for language teaching and learning. *ReCALL* 17: 163–78.

Oliver, M. and K. Trigwell. 2005. Can "blended learning" be redeemed? *E-Learning* 2, no. 1: 17–26. Accessed January 2012. http://www. luispitta.com/mie/Blended_Learning_2005.pdf.

Pena-Sanchez, R. and R. C. Hicks. 2006. Faculty perceptions of communications channels: A survey. *International Journal of Innovation and Learning* 3, no. 1: 45–62.

Rižnar, I. 2009. Blended language learning, *IBS Newsletter Porocevale.* Accessed January 2012. http://www.ibsporocevalec.si/ naslovnica/118-blended-language-learning.

Ruthven-Stuart, P. 2003. Integrating ICTs into a university language curriculum. Can it be done successfully? *Bulletin of Hokuriku University* 27: 159–176. Accessed January 2012. http://www.hokuriku-u.ac.jp/library/pdf/kiyo27/gai12.pdf.

Secande Life. Accessed January 2012. http://blendedlearning506no.wikispaces.com/Secande+Life.

Sharpe, R. et al. 2006. The undergraduate experience of blended e-learning: A review of UK literature and practice undertaken for the Higher Education Academy. Accessed January 2012. http://www.heacademy.ac.uk/assets/documents/research/literature_reviews/blended_elearning_full_review.pdf.

Silverwood, T. 2006. Blended learning made easy. *Learning*: 115–22. Accessed January 2012. http://www.chs.nihon-u.ac.jp/institute/human/kiyou/74/10.pdf.

Stracke, E. Conflicting voices: Blended learning in a German university foreign language classroom. In *Zusammenarbeiten: Eine Festschrift für Bernd Voss*, edited by M. Dúill, R. Zahn, and K. D. C. Höppner, 403–20. Bochum: AKS-Verlag, 2005. Also published in *Learner Autonomy 9: Autonomy in the classroom*, edited by L. Miller, 85–103. Dublin: Authentik, 2007.

———. 2007a.A road to understanding: A qualitative study into why learners drop out of a blended language learning (BLL) environment. *ReCALL* 19, no. 1: 57–78.

———. 2007b. Spotlight on blended language learning: A frontier beyond learner autonomy and computer assisted language learning. *Language Learning* October: 1–13. Accessed January 2012. http://independentlearning.org/ILA/ila07/files/ILA2007_036.pdf.